HOW TO BE AN
ART
REBEL

For Valentina – B.S.

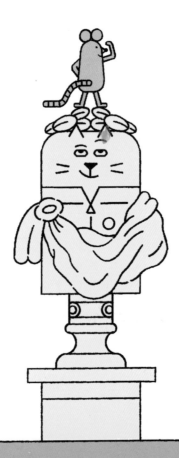

HOW TO BE AN ART REBEL

BEN STREET

ILLUSTRATED BY JAY DANIEL WRIGHT

I'm Leo, your art gallery guide. Get ready to have some fun! Because that's what being an art rebel is all about.

T&H

WHY YOU MUST BECOME AN ART REBEL

Leonardo da Vinci,
Mona Lisa, c. 1503–1519

PFFT!

Boring adults will tell you that art is SUPER serious.

But do you want to know the biggest art secret of all time? (Bigger than the secret of Mona Lisa's smile?)

ART-IS-FUN!

For thousands of years adults have been finding ways to describe art that makes it sound MYSTERIOUS and DIFFICULT, and something that only grown-ups know anything about.

That's just NONSENSE!

As you'll discover in this book,
art can be WACKY, EXPLOSIVE,
RUDE and VERY BADLY BEHAVED.

Art can make us think about scary
things like DEATH, and what it
feels like to be HAPPY. It can tell
us STORIES, challenge our IDEAS,
and make us feel UNDERSTOOD.

So if you want to ENJOY art,
it's time to REBEL.

To be a true art rebel you need to:

1 Make up your own mind—don't
   let adults tell you what to think.

2 Look at art from a different angle—
   stand on your head if you have to.

3 Don't worry about getting anything
   wrong—there are no right answers!

Always have fun.
And be weird.

Your art rebel training starts here...

CONTENTS

Ooof. "Surrealism?" "Abstract?"
All sounds like hard work, doesn't it?

Adults can put people off art by using
serious-sounding words, but you'll see I've
added some helpful notes so you get the idea.

PORTRAITS

PORTRAITS

You know how adults make fun of you for fixing up your selfies with filters? Well, that's NOTHING compared to what people used to go through to get a good picture.

Centuries ago, you couldn't scroll through a whole bunch of photos and delete all the BAD ones—there was no such thing as photos.

If people wanted to show themselves off to the world they had to hire an artist to paint a PORTRAIT of them.

Unknown artist, Chinese imperial portrait, possibly of Empress Dowager Cixi, *c.* 1835–1908

Unknown artist, A Mughal empress, c. 1800-1899

Unknown artist, Early Portrait of Naser al-Din Shah, c. 1850

Workshop of Rogier van der Weyden, Portrait of Isabella of Portugal, c. 1450

Hans Holbein the Younger, Hermann von Wedigh III, 1532

Emperors and empresses, kings and queens, shahs, merchants and dukes all had portraits specially made to show how NOBLE and important they were.

They dressed up in their best frocks and loads of jewelry to show people who was BOSS.

The truth is, some portraits aren't really real at all...

Famous, powerful people are some of the absolute biggest portrait fakers EVER.

Napoleon Bonaparte, the 19th-century leader of France, was SUCH a diva that he refused to even pose for this very impressive portrait.

Jacques-Louis David, Napoleon crossing the Alps at the Great Saint Bernard Pass, late 18th–early 19th century

The artist Jacques-Louis David only had a couple of hours with Napoleon as his sitter, who was a grumpy pain in the butt. In the end, David's son had to sit on a ladder, in one of Napoleon's old uniforms, so his dad could finish the painting.

And that was only the start of the fakery...

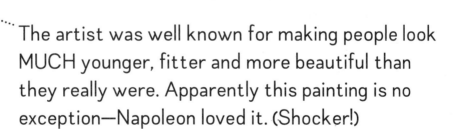

Just look at those wild stormy skies, the wind in Napoleon's cape and the horse's mane! Except that the real battle was on a mild, sunny day and Napoleon wore a very sensible buttoned coat.

The artist was well known for making people look MUCH younger, fitter and more beautiful than they really were. Apparently this painting is no exception—Napoleon loved it. (Shocker!)

Woah! A beautiful wild horse rearing up under Napoleon as he charges into battle. Very impressive. However, in the real-life battle Napoleon followed behind the army a few days later on a mule. Not quite so glam.

In the olden days, a portrait was how the world saw and remembered you. And before smartphone filters, people had to ask the artist to give them a bit of a—ahem—makeover.

Artists were usually happy to play along with all the fakery. Their delighted customers would tell all their rich friends— which meant more work and more money!

Look at the way the famous Dutch painter Anthony van Dyck painted his wife, Mary. The first thing you see is that dress—just look at it!

How do you even get paint to gleam and crinkle like silk? (By spending absolutely aaaages on it, that's how.)

But remember—this is a picture of a real-life person. Which makes you think— was Lady van Dyck's skin really that smooth? Were her fingers so long and elegant? And did she always walk around the house in pearls?

We will never know...

Anthony van Dyck, Mary, Lady van Dyck, *c.* 1640

Now when you're walking around a room full of very serious old portraits, you can imagine the sitters making their demands on the artist:

Make my jawline a bit more defined and my waist slimmer!

Hans Holbein the Younger, Portrait of Henry VIII, *c.* 1537

Frans Floris, Portrait of an Elderly Lady, 1558

I don't suppose you could paint me with a full set of gleaming white teeth?!

You can also imagine portraits for all the people around the world who never got portraits made because they were too poor to afford them.

They lived at the same time as all these kings and queens, growing the food and building the cities and doing all the important things. What thanks do they get, huh?!

Well, eventually some artists did become more interested in painting ordinary people. But because the sitters didn't need flattering, they didn't get the same beautifying treatment.

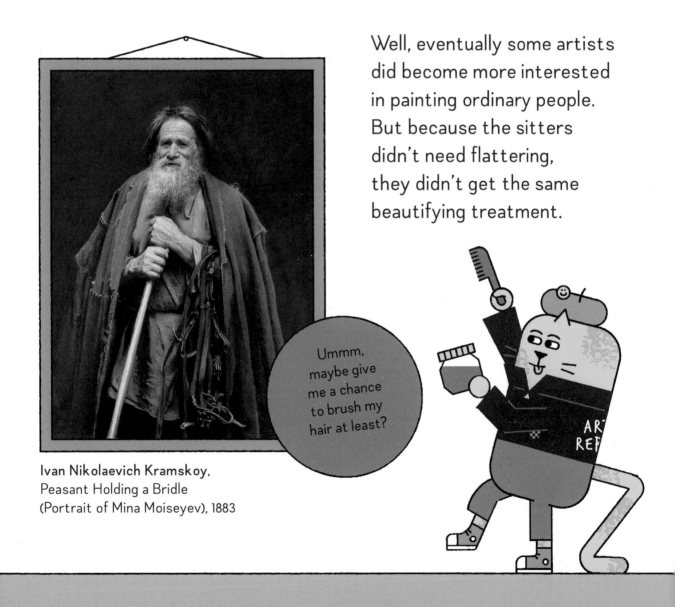

Ummm, maybe give me a chance to brush my hair at least?

Ivan Nikolaevich Kramskoy,
Peasant Holding a Bridle
(Portrait of Mina Moiseyev), 1883

17

Even if a portrait is fairly true to life, it can still tell us something about how a person would like to be seen.

Ignatius Sancho was a Black British writer, composer and shopkeeper in the 1700s, who was famous for his intelligence and wit. But his life was not easy.

He was born on a slave ship, and as a child he was forced to work as a slave for a rich London family. He ran away and convinced the Duke of Montagu to employ him.

When the fashionable portrait artist Thomas Gainsborough visited the Duke, he painted a portrait of Sancho too.

The gold trim on Sancho's waistcoat tells us that he is an important member of a noble household, not a servant.

Sancho is pictured on his own and without his employer, the Duke. He is a free man who is paid for his work.

His hand-in-waistcoat pose says, "I am a gentleman and a leader."

Thomas Gainsborough,
Ignatius Sancho, 1768

During the 18th century, most pictures of Black men in the U.K. showed them as slaves. So this portrait showed everyone what Sancho knew to be true: that all men are equal.

Nowadays we can easily use phone cameras to take our own selfies. But in the past, only artists could create SELF-PORTRAITS.

They often included CLUES in the picture that revealed who they really were. What do you notice in this painting?

Tropical plants and animals? Yes! She's from Mexico and very proud of her country, including all its lovely trees, bugs and furry animals.

Dark hair on her face? Absolutely! She loved her strong natural beauty.

Painful-looking thorny necklace? Good eye, reader! She had lots of health problems and wanted to show us the pain she felt every day.

Frida Kahlo, Untitled (Self-portrait with thorn necklace and hummingbird), 1940

Frida Kahlo's self-portrait is a different kind of pretending. She probably never sat in a jungle with a cat and a monkey on her shoulders. But these clues show us her real thoughts and feelings.

Arise, rebel master of portraits! It's time to head on to...

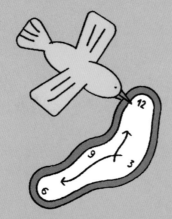

SURREALISM

SURREALISM

Have you ever sort of remembered a dream after you've woken up and tried explaining it to someone at breakfast?

Leonora Carrington, Self-Portrait, 1937–1938

A Surrealist painting looks like a dream.
And to make something look like a dream,
you have to make it seem mostly normal.

Normal room, normal chair,
normal(ish) rocking horse...

Then just add something not normal.
Something that doesn't belong there.
Maybe a hyena.

Because that's what dreams are full of.
Things that are out of place.

The thing is: we all dream.
Bus drivers.
Dentists.
Sergeant majors.
TEACHERS.

Adults do it just as much as anyone else. They have weird
stuff in their heads too, they just like to pretend that they don't.

So although it might feel like it's just you who has weird dreams,
they are one of the things we all have in common.

When we're awake, we get so used to pretending to be sensible and not seeing things in our own wonderfully weird ways.

The great thing about art is that it doesn't have to be sensible AT ALL.

You can see things in art that could only really exist in dreams...

...like this horrifying cup of tea.
Ewwww ewwwww, I can feel all the hair in my mouth!

Oh wait. Kkaarrgghh... that's a hairball. My bad.

Meret Oppenheim, Object
(Lunch in fur), 1936

The Surrealists were very eccentric adults who never learned to be all proper and boring.

They liked to let their minds wander to see what ideas they could come up with.

Sometimes they put a paintbrush or a pencil in their hand and just started moving it without trying to draw anything in particular. They called it "automatism"— a very serious adult word for doodling.

Joan Miró was the doodling MASTER. Second only to me, really.

Joan Miró, Harlequin's Carnival, 1924-1925

ART REBEL

What can you see in Miró's painting? There are no right answers, it's just a jumble of the inside of his brain!

(If an adult pretends they have
the right answer, you can
tell them from me that
they're a big stinking liar.)

Anyway, I can see...
a moon, a ladder, a guitar,
some snaky squiggles,
a devil monkey and a very
weird goat-kangaroo-bear.
And a horn! What about you?

The Surrealists made some great art but they also loved parties, dressing up and doing weird things in public to freak out all the fussy, uptight adults.

It sounds much more fun than most adults' lives—especially back then, when people fainted in shock if you buttoned your shirt wrong (probably).

So, the big secret about the Surrealists is ... they were really more like kids than adults. They just wanted to be silly, have fun, do weird and exciting things—in art and in life.

Philippe Halsman, *Salvador Dalí, 1954*

Top Surrealist artist Salvador Dalí was SUPER into playing around with his moustache. This, and his *Lobster Telephone*, an old-fashioned telephone with a lobster for a handle, goes to show that the Surrealists just wanted to have fun!

Surrealism might seem REALLY arty and serious, but it's not at all. You can be a Surrealist right now.

Honestly. It'll take five minutes, and you can tell your parents you can't possibly help with chores right now because you're being an artist.

1 Think of two objects that don't belong with one another and draw them fitting together.

2 Keep a piece of paper next to your bed. When you wake up, try to draw your dream before it fades away.

3 Close your eyes and draw for a minute straight. See what strange things comes out of the depths of your brain!

4 Do something weird and fun in front of other people. Walk like a crab, wear shoes on your hands, anything you like.

Way to get surreal!
Put on your lobster hat and we'll sashay over to...

ANCIENT SCULPTURE

ANCIENT SCULPTURE

Ever been through a museum
full of old statues and thought,
"Something's missing?"

And then realized it's
the person's HEAD?!

Ancient statues have been
around for THOUSANDS of years.
And just like other very old things,
they're not in perfect condition.

They get bumped and pieces
fall off. Anything that sticks out.
Their noses, their ears.
(Even their private parts.)

Unknown artist, Roman female torso, version of
a (lost) Greek statue of a goddess, *c.* 420-400 BCE

You might also have noticed that adults are very serious about old statues. "Oh, but it's CLASSICAL ART," they say. "It's from ANTIQUITY!"

If they're so great, why do pieces of them keep falling off? And why do they all look so GRAY?

Well, they used to look LIKE THIS:

The ancient Greeks and Romans used to paint their statues in wild colors. They were usually of gods or rulers, like Emperor Augustus here.

They painted them to look more exciting than ordinary people. Centuries later, boring adults who thought the colors looked a bit weird scrubbed them all away. So the statues looked nice and gray and SERIOUS. What a shame.

Unknown artist, Polychrome reconstruction of Augustus of Prima Porta, *c.* 20 BCE

If you think the colors of these statues were crazy, wait until you hear how crazy the stories they tell are!

Once upon a time, Actaeon was out hunting deer and saw the goddess Artemis washing herself in the river. With no clothes on.

He tried to sneak away after taking a look, but Artemis caught him looking. And she was upset. (As she should be!)

So Artemis turned Actaeon into a deer. And when his hunting dogs sniffed him, guess what? They gobbled him up.

The End.

There are tons of weird, incredible stories told through old gray statues. Once you know their secrets, they start to come alive!

Unknown artist, Artemis, Goddess of the Hunt, *c.* 5th-4th centuries BCE

If you thought that story was gruesome, try this:

Laocoön was an elderly priest (with a very muscly body) who lived in the city of Troy.

The Trojans (people from Troy) were sent a giant wooden horse as a present from their enemies, the Greeks.

How nice.

Except the horse was actually full of soldiers waiting to kill them. Worst. Present. EVER.

Unknown artist,
Statue of Laocoön and
His Sons, *c.* 40–30 BCE

Because Laocoön had warned his fellow Trojans of the imminent danger, the gods weren't too happy with him. You see, the gods were on the side of the Greeks.

The ancient gods were like bullies. But unlike normal, annoying bullies, they had unlimited magical powers.

They sent some snakes to kill Laocoön and his sons, which they did. Horribly.

Now let's get away from these horrible gods. Onward!

STILL LIFE

STILL LIFE

Jan van Huysum, Flowers in a Terracotta Vase, 1734

Adults love things like this. "How lovely," they say.

If the artist could hear that, he'd bonk them on the head. Here's why.

One day, Jan van Huysum bought some flowers so he could paint a picture of them. But it took him so long, they turned brown and died. So he bought some more.

Then he bought some grapes.
But he took so long painting them, they turned brown too.
And started to stink.

Pretty soon, Jan was at the market every other day, buying more and more flowers and grapes and eggs.

Once Jan was finally finished, he showed the painting to a friend. And what did he say?

"Lovely!" So Jan bonked him on the head.

I'm guessing, anyway. Wouldn't you? I mean, look at the detail in the painting opposite.

No fruit, just flowers. Every one of them as sharp as the reflection in a mirror.

This painting isn't lovely—it's positively DAZZLING!

Clara Peeters, *Still life with cheeses, almonds and pretzels, c.* 1615

A painting like this is called a "still life."

Whichever adult came up with that needs a medal for the
most boring name ever. Because still lifes are chock-full
of symbols and messages.

One thing many people love is cheese.
And Clara Peeters was one of the best cheese painters ever.
It's not easy being a cheese painter.
Because, 1) mice love cheese.
And 2) after a while, cheese begins to stink.

Back when Clara was at work, nearly every artist around was a man. That's because most people thought women were only supposed to have babies and do the cooking, not make art. Clara thought that was ridiculous.

She got pretty tired of people thinking her paintings must be by a man. So, in this painting she made sure everyone knew who it was by.

First she wrote her name on the knife...

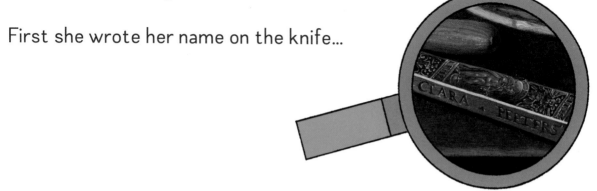

...and then she painted her own reflection in the jug. That's her, saying: "Look! I'm not a man, I'm Clara."

And also:
"This cheese has definitely gone bad. Gross."

Still lifes aren't all lovely.
Sometimes they tell us about the unlovely things in life.

Ori Gersht froze real flowers and then blew them up
so that they would shatter into tiny pieces.

His super-fast camera catches the explosion in mid-air.

Ori uses his still life to tell us how precious life is.
And how easy it is to destroy it.

See, with a still life, you need to look very carefully to find
out what it's really about. And it's never quite what it seems.

Ori Gersht, Blow Up 04, 2007

Pieter Claesz's still life painting is full of secret messages, called symbols, about how short life is. Depressing or what?!

Take his violin, for example.
The secret message it is sending you says, "Everyone loves a tune, but even music has to end. So enjoy it while it lasts." (Unless you're really bad at the violin, in which case, enjoy it when it's over.)

Pieter Claesz, Vanitas with Violin and Glass Ball, 1628

Looks like someone's been trying to fix this old watch, then dumped it on the table. We might try to work out how time works, but we never will. Get it?

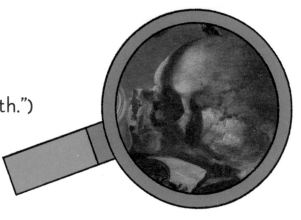

Yikes, a skull is never a good sign, is it? Guess what a skull is a symbol of. (Clue: it starts with D and it rhymes with "Beth.")

Just like Clara, Pieter put himself in his own painting. It's even more show-offy to use a curved mirror so you can see the whole room. But the mirror looks a bit like a bubble—as if it could pop at any minute. It means that Pieter knows that even his amazing talents won't last forever.

The moral of the story is that still lifes are not quite what they seem. So the next time an adult tells you how lovely they are, you know what to say.

Enough of these still lifes! It's time to get rude...

NUDE ART

NUDE ART

Sandro Botticelli, *Birth of Venus, c.* 1485

Adults behave very seriously in art galleries. Haven't they noticed all the naked people? There are TONS.

Take David and Venus here, for example. They're as naked as freshly-born babies! But they don't look much like the kind of people I know. In fact, they don't look like real people at all. They're a bit … posey.

Michelangelo, David, 1501–1504

Jean-Auguste-Dominique Ingres, La Grande Odalisque, 1814

The same applies to this woman above—
her bottom looks so soft, it's as if it
has been touched up with makeup.

This just goes to show that the way
people pose for photos today, trying
to look perfect, is nothing new.
People have been doing it for centuries!

But why? It's something we need
to get to the bottom of…

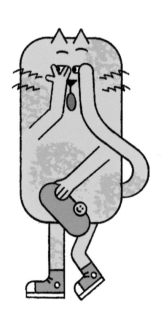

Back in the olden days, artists could only get away with painting pictures of naked people if their subjects came from the Bible (like David from page 52, who fought a giant called Goliath) or from mythology (Venus was an ancient Roman goddess).

Religious stories and myths = good influence.
Everyday naked people = bad influence.

So when Gustave Caillebotte painted this picture of a man getting out of the bath, people thought he was an art rebel!

Compared with the polished nudes that came before, Caillebotte's nude is hairy, sopping wet and has no idea he's being painted.

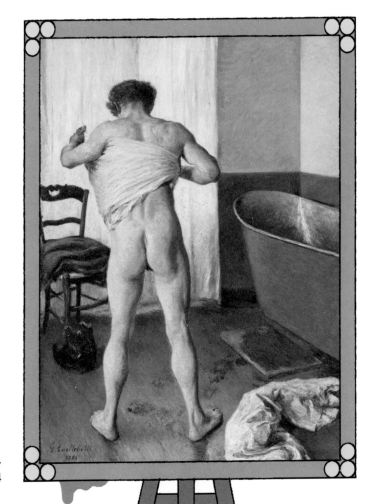

Gustave Caillebotte,
Man at His Bath, 1884

The thing is, there's no right
or wrong way for a body
to look.

Some us have big bellies.
Some of us don't.
Some of us have long,
skinny necks.
Some of us don't.
Some of us use
birds to cover
up our private parts...

AND ALL OF THE
REST OF US DON'T.
(Sorry, but that
is pretty weird.)

Agnolo Bronzino, Portrait of Nano Morgante,
before 1553

It's not unusual to want to look
our best—especially if we know
our nude body will be on show...

Marc Quinn's nude sculpture of the artist Alison Lapper was made especially for public display on the Fourth Plinth in London's Trafalgar Square.

Lapper was born without arms and with shortened legs, and has had to overcome the challenges of her physical disability, as well as other people's discomfort around her.

By carving her figure out of marble, Quinn makes Lapper's naked body look like a goddess's, without looking posey.

Marc Quinn, Alison Lapper Pregnant, 2005

Bhupen Khakhar, You Can't Please All, 1981

Art with naked people reminds us that, no matter who we are, or what our lives are like, we're actually very similar to one another.

Bhupen Khakhar painted this picture of himself in the nude just before he announced his sexuality as a gay man. This painting was his coming-out. Even though his way of life didn't please all, Khakhar's nude bottom shows us he had pride in his identity.

That's enough butts for now!
Let's get totally abstract, man...

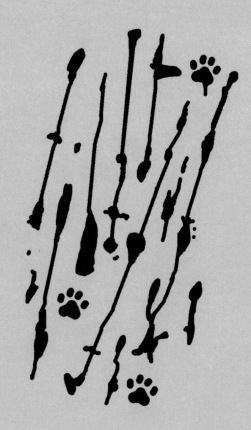

ABSTRACT ART

ABSTRACT ART

Sometimes words simply can't explain how you feel about a place. Sometimes, what you need is a picture to tell the story.

When Joan Mitchell painted this, she was thinking of a particular place: Minnesota. But she didn't want to paint exactly what Minnesota looks like. She could just take a photo—anyone can do that.

Instead, Joan wanted her painting to show her memories of it, including the wind blowing across a corn field.

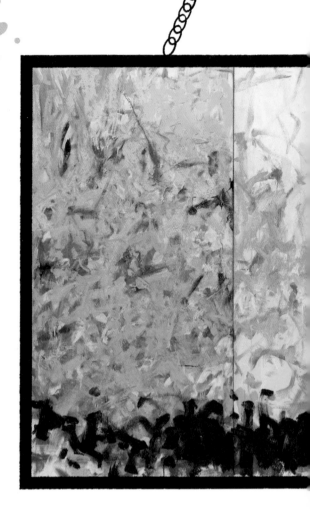

Joan Mitchell, Minnesota, 1980

What do you think the weather was like—hot and sunny, or horribly rainy?

How do you think she felt about Minnesota—happy and excited to be there, or a bit blah?

See—there's a lot you can read in a painting without any words at all!

But wait a minute. What do you paint if you don't want your picture to look like anything?

Imagine something you could never see in real life. Like a spooky feeling.

Piet Mondrian, Composition No. III, with Red, Blue, Yellow, and Black, 1929

Piet Mondrian wanted to show in his painting that, although we live in a physical world, there are some pretty interesting things we can't see, that we might describe as "spiritual."

By arranging shapes and colors together in a pleasing way, Mondrian was doing exactly what Islamic artists had done centuries before him. The patterns created with tiles at the Alhambra Palace show that all things—both physical and spiritual—exist in perfect harmony.

Unknown artist, Tile from the Alhambra Palace, Andalusia, Spain, 14th century

If abstract art can show us something as complicated as the balance between the spiritual and physical worlds, what else could it show—a disgusting smell? Or even... MUSIC?

Here's a question for you: what does music look like?
I don't mean a musical instrument. I mean MUSIC!

Wassily Kandinsky thought it might look
something like this picture.

And if you really try—you can almost hear it.
It's a bit noisy and crazy and hard to sing along to.
You couldn't whistle it while waiting for the bus.
But it is a bit like music.

Wassily got very annoyed by people saying things like,
"That part looks like a spider's web." Or, "Wow, a fireworks
display in space." "No, you idiots! It's abstract!" he replied.

You get his point. It isn't of anything at all.

Wassily Kandinsky,
Black Lines, 1913

Just like Wassily, Barbara Hepworth made art that wasn't
of anything. So don't go telling her that this looks like
a hazelnut with a hole in it, or an alien guitar.

Barbara made sculptures that showed how the landscape
felt to her. She loved the English coastline, especially
Cornwall, where she lived.

And if you look carefully, you might see shapes
that remind you of crashing waves.
Or pebbles.
Or hills and caves.

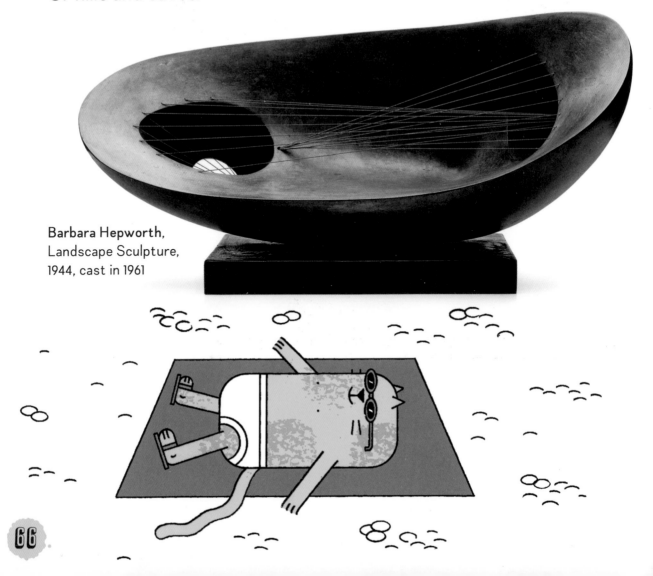

Barbara Hepworth,
Landscape Sculpture,
1944, cast in 1961

You could make some abstract art yourself.
Think of something that you couldn't photograph.

1 Maybe the feeling of being really hungry.

2 Or the shock of jumping into a really cold swimming pool.

3 Or the smell of a really horrendous fart.

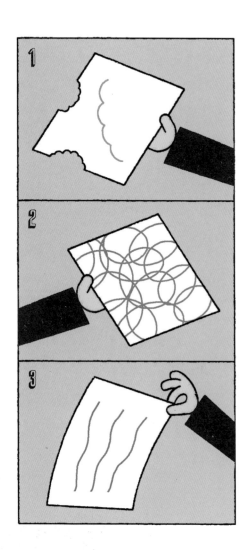

And create some art that shows that. It's not easy
to make something that doesn't look like anything.
Art doesn't have to be OF anything to be INTERESTING.

Enough of all this abstract business,
it's time to get contemporary!

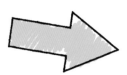

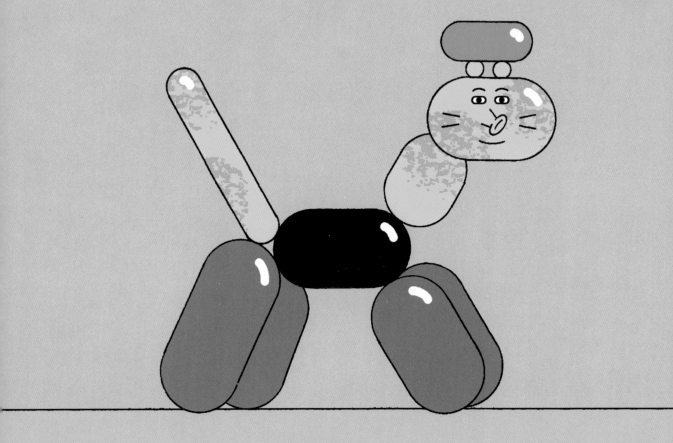

CONTEMPORARY ART

CONTEMPORARY ART

Contemporary art can be anything.
"What a bunch of nonsense," adults like
to say.

(And sometimes contemporary art really
is a bunch of nonsense. Gustav Metzger's
Auto-Destructive Art installation at
Tate Modern in London was so convincing,
the cleaner threw it away!)

But adults who say contemporary art is
nonsense are just forgetting something...

That we're all different.
So the art we make is different, too.

One day, Yayoi Kusama decided
she'd invite other people to
make art together.

First she painted a
room completely white.
Then she let anyone
stick stickers wherever
they wanted.

Yayoi Kusama, The obliteration room, 2002-present

Adults might stand back, scratch their chins and say, "You're not supposed to do that."

But Yayoi wants us to get involved, so we can all share her way of seeing the world. Even if it means bending the rules.

What is your favorite thing about the area where you live?
Maybe it's a cool building?
Or a colorful wall covered in street art?
Something you can't imagine a place without.
Now imagine someone destroyed it.
How would you feel?

One day, a beautiful statue in Iraq was blown to bits.
On purpose. By people who didn't care how anyone felt about it.
It was an ancient statue of a lamassu—a half-man, half-bull,
winged god. This sculpture is almost the same as that one.
But there's a big difference ... it's made out of old date syrup cans.

Michael Rakowitz chose a material that is instantly
recognizable to people from Iraq, because the
lamassu belonged to the whole country.
It took 10,500 date syrup
cans to make this sculpture.

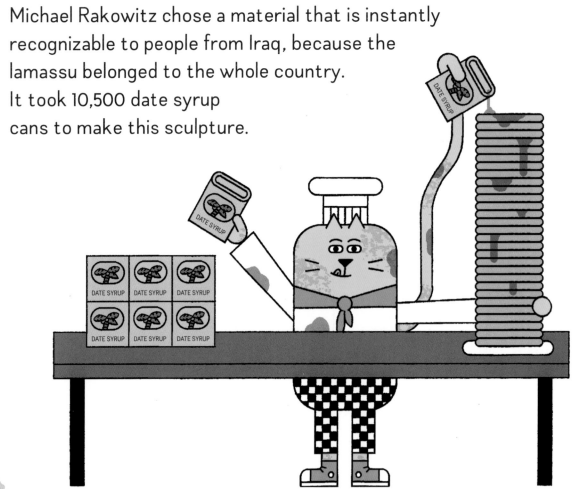

Michael Rakowitz describes his sculpture as a ghost. He wants it to haunt us so that we never forget the lost lamassu.

Michael Rakowitz,
The Invisible Enemy
Should Not Exist,
2018

73

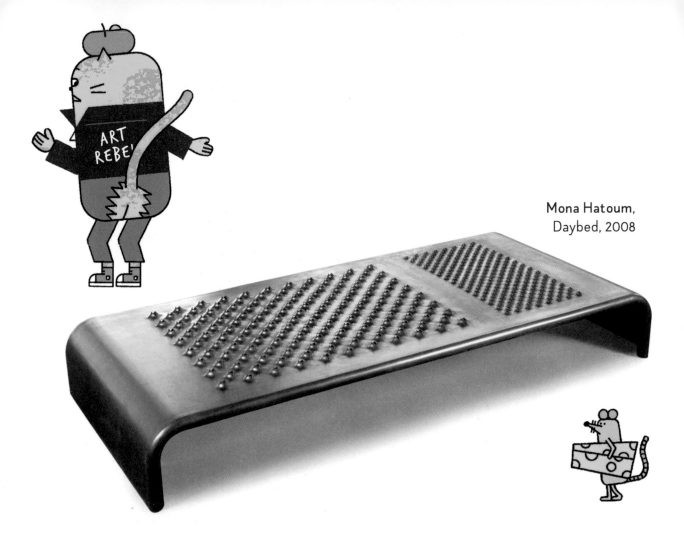

Mona Hatoum,
Daybed, 2008

Even though it looks like a bench, this giant cheese grater
is not made for sitting on. The artist Mona Hatoum reminds
us that being in public can be uncomfortable for anyone.
Even adults.

Because here's the biggest secret of all...
All artists are HUMAN BEINGS.
They aren't aliens or monsters. Even if they might sometimes
look a bit like them. Just like you and me (especially me),
they aren't always serious. Sometimes they're silly.
Or uncomfortable. Or ecstatically happy.
Or HUNGRY!

Tom Friedman made a giant sculpture of a pizza that looks so
real you might want to take a slice. Sometimes when I'm hungry,
all I can think about is food. In fact, that's most of my average day.
I think Tom feels that way too.

So when an adult tries to tell you what art's all about,
just keep nodding your head and saying,
"Oh really? Wow, how clever you are!"

But PLEASE, PLEASE don't
tell them how fun it is!
It's our big, amazing secret.

Tom Friedman,
Untitled (Pizza), 2013

GLOSSARY

ABSTRACT ART

Art that doesn't look like anything. Abstract art is usually lots of shapes, colors, or squiggly things, just as long as it's not realistic.

ANCIENT

From a very, very, very, VERY long time ago.

ANTIQUITY

Ancient times. Everything before the Middle Ages is described as being "from antiquity."

AUTOMATISM

A way of making art automatically, without thinking about it.

CANVAS

A piece of cloth used for painting on, which is usually stretched over a wooden frame or stuck onto something flat.

CAST

A sculpture made from a mold. Usually a metal like bronze is melted down, poured into a mold, and left to cool down and harden. Break the mold off, and bingo—you have one shiny bronze cast.

CLASSICAL ART

The art that the ancient Greeks and Romans made—think super-realistic marble sculptures made during the 5th and 4th centuries BCE.

CONTEMPORARY ART

Art made recently—it could have been made today, yesterday, or in the past ten years or so. It's hard to put a date to it because time just keeps ticking...

INSTALLATION

An artwork that is designed for a specific space. Yayoi Kusama's *The obliteration room* (pages 70-71) is an installation.

MARBLE

One of the most popular materials used by sculptors. Cold, white, very heavy and difficult to chip into, but looks very nice.

MODEL

A person who poses for an artist.

PAINTING

A flat picture made using paint.

PHOTOGRAPH

A picture taken with a camera. Before you were born, cameras had a roll of film inside them instead of microchips and electronic wizardry.

PORTRAIT

A picture of a specific person. More often than not, portraits show a person looking their best, or better than their best.

SCULPTURE

A three-dimensional work of art. Usually stands on a pedestal. Sometimes you can walk all the way around it, sometimes not.

SELF-PORTRAIT

A picture of the artist by the artist. You might be surprised to know that not all self-portraits have to be realistic—they can be totally abstract, or full of symbols.

SITTER

The person having their portrait made.

STILL LIFE

A picture of things sitting still. Usually the types of things you'd find on a dining table—food, cutlery, a bunch of flowers, a book, a skull...

STUDIO

Where an artist makes their work.

SURREALISM

An art movement made up of painters, poets, photographers and filmmakers. The Surrealists used art to explore their dreams and loved digging up ideas from the part of the brain called "the subconscious."

LIST OF ARTWORKS

Dimensions of works are given in centimeters (and inches), height before width.

page 37
Unknown artist
Artemis, Goddess of the Hunt,
5th-4th centuries BCE
Marble, height 200 (78³/₄)
Louvre, Paris. Photo Josse/Scala, Florence

page 38-39
Unknown artist
Statue of Laocoön and His Sons, c. 40-30 BCE
208 x 163 x 112 (82 x 64¹/₄ x 44¹/₈)
Vatican Museums, Rome. Photo Adam
Eastland/Alamy Stock Photo

page 42
Jan van Huysum
Flowers in a Terracotta Vase, 1734
Oil on canvas, 81 x 60.6 (31⁷/₈ x 23⁷/₈)
Private collection. Photo The Picture Art
Collection/Alamy Stock Photo

page 44
Clara Peeters
*Still life with cheeses, almonds and
pretzels*, c. 1615
Oil on panel, 34.5 x 49.5 (13⁵/₈ x 19¹/₂)
Mauritshuis, The Hague

page 45
Clara Peeters
*Still life with cheeses, almonds and
pretzels* (details), c. 1615
Oil on panel, 34.5 x 49.5 (13⁵/₈ x 19¹/₂)
Mauritshuis, The Hague

page 47
Ori Gersht
Blow Up 04, 2007
Light Jet, 240 x 180 (94¹/₂ x 70⁷/₈)
© Ori Gersht. All rights reserved,
DACS/Artimage 2020

page 48
Pieter Claesz
Vanitas with Violin and Glass Ball, 1628
Oil on oak, 35.9 x 59 (14¹/₄ x 23¹/₄)
Germanisches Nationalmuseum, Nuremberg
akg-images

page 49
Pieter Claesz
Vanitas with Violin and Glass Ball
(details), 1628
Oil on oak, 35.9 x 59 (14¹/₄ x 23¹/₄)
Germanisches Nationalmuseum, Nuremberg

page 52
Left
Michelangelo
David, 1501-1504
Marble, height 426.72 (168)
Accademia Gallery, Florence

Right
Sandro Botticelli
Birth of Venus, c. 1485
Tempera on canvas, 172.5 x 278.5 (68 x 109³/₄)
Uffizi Museum, Florence

page 53
Jean-Auguste-Dominique Ingres
La Grande Odalisque, 1814
Oil on canvas, 91 x 162 (35⁷/₈ x 63⁷/₈)
Louvre, Paris

page 54
Gustave Caillebotte
Man at His Bath, 1884
Oil on canvas, 144.8 x 114.3 (57 x 45)
Museum of Fine Arts, Boston
Photo © 2020 Museum of Fine Arts, Boston.
All rights reserved/Scala, Florence

page 55
Agnolo Bronzino
Portrait of Nano Morgante
(*The dwarf Morgante*), before 1553
Oil on canvas, 150 x 98 (59¹/₈ x 38⁵/₈)
Uffizi Gallery, Florence. Photo Scala,
Florence

page 56
Marc Quinn
Alison Lapper Pregnant, 2005
Marble, 355 x 180 x 260 (139⁷/₈ x
70⁷/₈ x 102³/₈)
© Marc Quinn. Photo Nic Hamilton/
Alamy Stock Photo © Marc Quinn.

page 57
Bhupen Khakhar
You Can't Please All, 1981
Oil on canvas, 175.6 x 175.6 (69¹/₄ x 69¹/₄)
Tate. © Chemould Prescott Road,
and the Estate of Bhupen Khakhar

page 60-61
Joan Mitchell
Minnesota, 1980
Oil on canvas, 260.4 x 621.4 (102¹/₂ x 244⁵/₈)
Collection Fondation Louis Vuitton
© Estate of Joan Mitchell

page 62
Piet Mondrian
*Composition No. III, with Red, Blue,
Yellow, and Black*, 1929
Oil on canvas, 50 x 50.2 (19³/₄ x 19⁷/₈)
Private collection. Photo © Christie's
Images/Bridgeman Images

page 63
Unknown artist
Tile from the Alhambra Palace, Andalusia,
Spain, 14th century
Photo Joser Pizarro/Shutterstock

page 65
Wassily Kandinsky
Black Lines, 1913
Oil on canvas, 129.4 x 131.1 (51 x 51⁵/₈)
Solomon R. Guggenheim Museum, New York
© 2020 The Solomon R. Guggenheim
Foundation/Art Resource, NY/ Scala,
Florence

page 66
Barbara Hepworth
Landscape Sculpture, conceived in 1944,
cast in 1961
Bronze with green patina and string,
66 x 31.8 (26 x 12⁵/₈)
Barbara Hepworth © Bowness. Photo
© Christie's Images/Bridgeman Images

page 70-71
Yayoi Kusama
The obliteration room, 2002-present
Furniture, white paint and dot stickers,
dimensions variable
Collaboration between Yayoi Kusama
and Queensland Art Gallery. Commissioned
Queensland Art Gallery. Gift of the artist
through the Queensland Art Gallery
Foundation 2012. Queensland Art Gallery
| Gallery of Modern Art. © Yayoi Kusama.
Photo Mark Sherwood, QAGOMA

page 73
Michael Rakowitz
The Invisible Enemy Should Not Exist, 2018
10,500 Iraqi date syrup cans, metal frame,
length 426.7 (168)
© Michael Rakowitz. Photo Zefrog/
Alamy Stock Photo

page 74
Mona Hatoum
Daybed, 2008
Black finished steel, 31.5 x 219 x 98
(12¹/₂ x 86¹/₄ x 38⁵/₈)
© Mona Hatoum. Courtesy Galerie
Max Hetzler, Berlin | Paris. Photo Jörg
von Bruchhausen

page 75
Tom Friedman
Untitled (Pizza), 2013
Styrofoam and paint, 218.44 x 218.44 x 12.7
(86 x 86 x 5)
© Tom Friedman. Courtesy of the artist,
Luhring Augustine, New York, and Stephen
Friedman Gallery, London

BEN STREET is an art historian and writer based in London. He is the author of several books on art for various ages and has worked as an educator at the National Gallery and Dulwich Picture Gallery, London, and MoMA, New York.

JAY DANIEL WRIGHT is an award-winning illustrator based in Berlin. His illustrations appear in *Think and Make Like an Artist*.

Front cover illustration:
Leonardo da Vinci, *Mona Lisa, c.* 1503–1519

First published in the United States of America in 2021 by Thames & Hudson Inc., 500 Fifth Avenue, New York, New York 10110

How to Be an Art Rebel © 2021 Thames & Hudson Ltd

Text © 2021 Ben Street
Illustrations © 2021 Jay Daniel Wright

Edited by Alice Harman
Designed by Belinda Webster

Library of Congress Control Number 2020950189

ISBN 978-0-500-65164-3

Printed and bound in China by C & C Offset Printing Co. Ltd

MIX
Paper from responsible sources
FSC® C008047
www.fsc.org

Be the first to know about our new releases, exclusive content and author events by visiting
thamesandhudson.com
thamesandhudsonusa.com
thamesandhudson.com.au